T0114755

Golden Buttons

Published by
Luviri Press
P/Bag 201 Luwinga
Mzuzu 2
Malawi

ISBN   978-99960-96-81-5
eISBN   978-99960-60-50-2

Luviri Reprints no. 7

Luviri Press is represented outside Malawi by:
African Books Collective Oxford (order@africanbookscollective.com)

www.mzunipress.blogspot.com
www.africanbookscollective.com

Editorial assistance and cover: Daniel Neumann

Printed in Malawi by Baptist Publications, P.O. Box 444, Lilongwe

Golden Buttons

Christianity and Traditional Religion among the Tumbuka

Stephen Kauta Msiska

Luviri Press

Luviri Reprints no. 7
Mzuzu
2018

To my dear wife and children Dora T. Zumara

Linnaeus K. Msiska
Darwin K. Msiska*
Victoria K. Msiska
Jean K. Msiska*
Emily Nyasa Msiska*
Marion K. Msiska
Stephen Mazaza Msiska*
Christina K. Msiska
John Kauta
Ian Joshua Msiska*

(* "sleeping")

Luviri Reprints

Many books have been published on or in Malawi that are no longer available. While some of these books simply have run their course, others are still of interest for scholars and the general public. Some of the classics have been reprinted outside Malawi over the decades, and during the last two decades, first the Kachere Series and then other publishers have achieved "never out of stock status" by joining the African Books Collective's Print on Demand approach, but there are still a good number of books that would be of interest but are no longer in print.

The Luviri Reprint Series has taken up the task to make those books on or from Malawi, which are out of print but not out of interest, available again, through Print on Demand and therefore worldwide.

While the Luviri Reprint Series concentrates on Malawi, it is also interested in the neighbouring countries and even in those further afield.

Luviri Reprints publish the books as they originally were. Usually a new Foreword is added, and where appropriate, new information has been added. All such additions, mostly in footnotes, are marked by an asterisk (*).

The Editors

Series Editors' Preface

The Kachere Series is an initiative of the Department of Theology and Religious Studies at the University of Malawi. It aims to promote the emergence of a body of literature which will enable students and others to engage critically with religion in Malawi, its social impact and with the theological questions which it raises. An important starting point lies with the publication of essays and theses which until now have been inaccessible to all but the most dedicated specialist. It is also hoped, however, that the development of theological scholarship in Malawi will stimulate the writing of many new books. General works with popular appeal are published as *Kachere Books,* with Mambo Press in Gweru. Full-length academic treatises are published as *Kachere Monographs,* with CLAIM in Blantyre. Documents and essays, which are of value as sources for the study of religion in Malawi, can be published as *Kachere Texts,* also with CLAIM in Blantyre. This third branch of the Series provides a forum for the publication of a variety of texts: discussion papers, bibliographies, short biographical studies, documentation, theological essays etc. Here is the place not necessarily for the last word but perhaps for the first word on an important area of study.

It is with particular pleasure that we issue, in this small volume, essays written by a pioneer theologian. Stephen Kauta Msiska was one of the first Malawians to put pen to paper as a Christian theologian and we are confident that his work will prove to be of permanent importance. Distinctive in his writing is a profound, though not uncritical, sympathy with the traditional religion of his people combined with a passionate concern for authentic Christian discipleship. Moreover, Kauta will be remembered not only as theologian but also as martyr. For he was one of those whose integrity as a Christian pastor brought him into collision with the one-party system of the post-independence era and who was forced to live in premature retirement under threat of his life. This book therefore makes accessible to a wider circle the fruits of Stephen Kauta's rich scholarship, pastoral sensitivity and suffering for the gospel's sake. The first essay was first published in 1969 in the Lesotho journal

Ministry Vol. 9 No. 1, pp. 3-11. The second was published in an abbreviated form in 1996 in Kachere Book No. 3 *Christianity in Malawi: A Sourcebook* (Gweru: Mambo Press), pp. 69-79. We are grateful to Dr Jack Thompson of the University of Edinburgh for helping us to trace the first essay, to Rev Dr Fergus Macpherson for generously agreeing to write the Foreword, to Mr Augustine W.C. Msiska and Mrs Fulata Moyo for advice on Tumbuka orthography, and to the CCAP Synod of Livingstonia for permission to reproduce on the cover their photograph of Rev Kauta Msiska. Our hope is that this book will offer "golden buttons" to many readers who are asking the questions which the author has boldly attempted to address.

Kachere Series Editors,
Zomba, Easter 1997

Foreword

Stephen Kauta Msiska was born in the early years of the twentieth century, probably in 1914, when the presence of powerful intruders from Europe had already roughly changed the pattern of life for many of the peasant communities to the west of Lake Malawi. The British drive for conquest, spearheaded by Sir Harry Johnston, had brought under armed control a large region known as the British Central Africa Protectorate: a region that had as neighbour on its western length the considerably larger region which Cecil Rhodes' British South Africa Company initially referred to as Northern Zambesia. While Stephen was still a toddler, the British administration in Nyasaland, like that of the BSAC, press ganged tens of thousands of men into war porterage in face of the extension of the European war (1914-1918) into the area of east and central Africa. The German forces in Tanganyika were confronting British forces in the northern reaches of what are now called Malawi and Zambia. That escalation created the real possibility of the tearing up of the Anglo-German Convention of 1890 which had drawn a flimsy frontier between the large areas forcibly annexed by agents of these two "imperial powers" during the so-called "partition of Africa". Henry Morton Stanley, the young American newsman who had "found Livingstone" near Lake Tanganyika at Ujiji In 1871, writing later, as a contemporary of the "carve up" of the continent by European "powers", declared that the "scramble" reminded him of how his "black followers used to run with gleaming knives for slaughtered game".[1]

Malawi, as now defined, had however shared a frontier also with the Portuguese colony of Mozambique which, like Angola, had been subjugated by those Iberian invaders in the years following the historic rounding of Africa's southern Cape in 1497 by Captain Vasco de Gama on his long voyage in search of a sea route to the Indies. Portuguese rule had been marked by much brutality, debauchery and by widespread slavery. David Livingstone had recorded his shock at conditions in their trading posts in Mozambique, at Tete and Senna,

---

[1]   Cit. R. Hall, *Stanley*, London: Collins, 1974, p. 265.

which in his eyes, were dens of all manner of immorality. Though Sir Harry Johnston had asserted that British rule was benevolent by comparison with Portugal's *ancient regime* in south-east Africa, he swiftly introduced the harsh and relentless taxation of all males which led to armed resistance and the wholesale burning of houses and grain-stores in many villages to "punish tax defaulters". In 1895 Chief Makanjira's capital, containing over 8,000 houses and with a population of "probably much more than 25,000 people" (as reported by Major Forbes who was in command of the operation) was totally destroyed.[2] Such wanton action provoked sharp protests from some missionaries and notably from the Scots missionaries in Blantyre in their periodical *Life and Work in British Central Africa*. For they foresaw "horrors that loom in the future of prison flogging, deportation, taxation ... irresponsible oppression of chiefs and people... the advent of a new slavery".[3] It would thus be impossible to consider the history of the region west of Lake Malawi, into which Stephen Kauta was born, without noting the magnitude of the impact, twenty years before his birth, of British armed power upon the lives of the whole local population. When, forty years later, the white dominated Central African Federation was imposed on Nyasaland and the two Rhodesias, African fears were justified by such memories. However, before that intrusion, there had come Christian missionaries, mainly from Scotland, in the years immediately after David Livingstone's death in 1873. It was as part of the harvest of that missionary enterprise that, in the fullness of time, the young man Msiska was to "give his heart to Jesus Christ" and go on to become an ordained minister of Word and Sacrament of the Church of Central Africa Presbyterian.

Given the Christian name Stephen, the youngster also inherited his father's nickname Kauta, which means in the Tumbuka language of

---

[2]   State Papers 1896, Major Edwards' Report, 27 December 1895, British Museum CC8013.

[3]   *Life and Work in British Central Africa*, October 1890, June 1892, March 1894; cit. F. Macpherson, *Anatomy of a Conquest*, London: Longman, 1981.

northern Malawi, "little bow". It was reportedly a nickname earned through prowess at hunting. Msiska is a clan name. One can perhaps indulge one's fancy by observing how this modest, gentle, long-suffering man, some of whose writings are offered in this small book, was indeed to be a "little bow" in the hand of his Lord, to protect and defend those he served from what Paul called, in his letter to Christians in Ephesus (6.16), "the fiery darts of the wicked".

I first met Stephen Kauta in April 1947, five months after arriving in Central Africa as a member of the United Missions in the Copperbelt of Northern Rhodesia. We found each other, so to speak, as we left a meeting of what was then called the District Council of the Church, and as our eyes met, we each discovered a new friend. Fifty years since then, I still count him as a very special person, one to whose quiet and radical goodness, sensitivity, sweetness, honesty, peace-making, humour and bright mirthfulness I have (as Americans might say), "resonated" with unclouded gladness and gratitude. The fact also of the deep love that binds him to Dora Nyauzumara, his sweetheart through joy and no less in suffering, has, as such wedded felicity must do, made him all the more precious as a friend. Being shorter a little in stature than his bride, he has often spoken of her, merrily, as *batali-batali ba ku Kenani* (the tall woman of Canaan). But the sight of white gravestones in front of their home at Chilulu, near Muhuju in the lower Henga valley south of Livingstonia, bespeaks something of the sore grief they have shared in the loss of two sons buried there, another son who died in Zambia and two daughters buried at the homes of their husbands. It also testifies to their shared assurance, as people whose creed includes explicitly belief "in the resurrection of the body and the life everlasting", that when their own time to "pass on" comes, those five dear ones will be waiting to welcome them.

Mission as Letting the Light Shine

As I read Stephen Kauta's manuscript in draft, it was as though he was speaking to me face to face, of a number of concerns, queries and convictions that have been his companions through most of his

11

life. In the section where he describes and criticises the assumption of some early missionaries that, in promoting Christianity, they must extirpate and ban all the beliefs and customs of those they sought to convert, he reminded me of what the late Alexander McAlpine (who had joined the Livingstonia Mission of the Free Church of Scotland in 1892) said to me fifty-four years later when I was about to sail for Africa. "My young friend, you know we made a terrible mistake when we first went out and we paid for it dearly in later years. We forgot that God was there first".

Stephen Kauta expresses his own awareness of their oversight thus: "When the Christian Gospel was first preached ... everything that was being done in connection with religion was suddenly branded as superstition, paganism and satanism by most people who came from the West, bringing in the Gospel..."; thus "The African has rightly thrown out his dirty, torn old shirt, but he has at the same time lost his golden buttons with it". Readers of this little book will be bound to realize how much the strategy of many foreign missionaries evoked in Stephen Kauta - and doubtless in very many more African people - a deep disquiet and set him thinking deeply about the nature of true Christianity.

The apparent outlawing and derogation of the immemorial heritage of spirituality in the worship and in the world-view of the communities from among which converts were being sought has, as Stephen Kauta believes, created a vacuum of deprivation. For example: many missionaries in seeking to teach Christian prayer at a time when they themselves were inevitably struggling to grasp languages totally new to them, would offer as the correct opening words a translation of "O God almighty" as *"Chiuta wa nkhongono zose"*. Equally inevitably such phrases would be given canonical status. Thus access for the "movement of the Spirit" would be restricted; and then the glorious inheritance of praise names for God (*vithokozo* in Chitumbuka) was banished and, by many local Christians, forgotten. Yet for their forebears, the High God had been *Kamanyi-manyi* - the All-knowing One; *Kajilengi* the self-created one; *Mziribanda* - the one without bounds, the all-embracing one; *Chiuta* - the great bow of heaven; *Chilera Balanda* - the nourisher of orphans; and many more. The first

12

section of this little book is full of fascinating insights into the thoughts and the speech of peoples who, in no sense, could be described as "atheists", i.e. people living without God.

Discipleship - True or Counterfeit

Perhaps the most insistent element in Stephen Kauta's own thought and in his work as a theological teacher, has been the concern to identify and define the means of enabling Christianity to be real and whole; his awareness of how often "religion" is shrunken to formality and conventional exercises, whereby the lips are left to do what instead should be translated into a way of life and of relationships radically different from "the way of the world". For him, therefore, faith must be "incarnational", simply because in Christ, "the Word was made flesh". Thus, for him, nothing must be allowed to divert attention from what Paul expressed epigrammatically in his long letter to Christians in Rome: "Do not be conformed to this world, but be transformed by the renewal of your minds, so that you may prove what is the will of God, what is good and acceptable and perfect." (Romans 12:2).

If we do not grasp what Stephen Kauta is striving after, in harmony with Christ's clear teaching, we cannot avoid the "backsliding" that has marked the life-style of so many nominal Christian believers around the world and down the ages. In consequence, we become, at best, "secret disciples", as is so neatly expressed in many of the great spiritual songs, to Malawian words and music, that make up the hymn book of the local churches - *Samu za Akristu*. Notable among them is a song beginning with the words: *Nga ndi Yayiro nkumchemani* - Like Jairus I am calling you to come to the home of my heart, where there is a trouble that has defeated me. For this song goes on to express this primary concern of our writer when it says that "in the worshipping congregation, I am a person, I can stand

13

upright with my head high, but back at home in my village, I am just a weak fool." (*Pa maungano ndiri munthu; ndiri mzereza m'kaya lane*).[4]

Bitter Fruits of Christian Disunity

The vital issue of letting our personal Christianity be real raises another question that has burdened unnumbered Christian hearts through the ages, to wit: What would have happened, or how would it have been, if missionaries, instead of transplanting their separate denominational institutions and practices, had simply gone forth to sow the seeds of the Gospel by deed and word, in that order? What has it been like to receive the Message from splintered denominations in lands for which the issues, that set Christians against other Christians in bitter controversy and often in open hatred, had nothing to do with the "divine-human encounter"? How can mainly Western churches work out their penitence for such a debilitating distortion of the biblical image of the followers of Jesus as a people living out in worship, in fellowship, service and reality what we sing about so carelessly in our many separated groups, "One Church, one Faith, one Lord"? Here Stephen Kauta would echo the words of the Sotho minister (ordained under Methodism) who told me with real passion of his conviction that, while people quarrel because that's how people are, we had done a great wrong in wrapping up the beautiful Gospel of Jesus in separate parcels and stamping the labels: Methodist or Seventh Day Adventist or Anglican or Roman Catholic or Reformed or whatever; thereby requiring the people of Africa to become these separated groups and so setting us against each other.

The situation in which Christians find themselves today is spotlighted at various points in Stephen Kauta's writing. "Christianity here", he declares, "is like an old car with rotten brakes - going down a hill to cross a rotten bridge.... Some one asks 'What is the future of Christianity in the village?'" And this is a question that can cause fear and trembling for Christians in many lands, and perhaps especially

---

[4]   For the full text of the hymn, with English translation, see K.R. Ross ed., *Christianity in Malawi: A Sourcebook*, Gweru: Mambo Press, 1996, p. 63.

where mammonism and acquisitive consumerist individualism effectively produce a popular and pervasive atheism. But this little book doesn't stop at such gloomy forebodings. Instead, we are offered a triumphant assurance that, since Christ is not dead but risen, "Christianity will never end... If we are to think of the future, the world is the battleground of good over evil and the training place of the children of God. It awaits the day when all wrong will be put right and truth will prevail". So, we all need to discover, as a friend in Scotland once said to me, that "The Church is not the company of the saved. It is the companions of the Saviour". And the word companions, in its Latin roots, means "bread fellows" or, let us say, fellow travellers with him who is indeed the Bread of Life. For Stephen Kauta, Christ is "all in all" so that he himself has lived as a peacemaker *(muphemaniski)*, one of those who should therefore be called "children of God".

You could describe Stephen Kauta as a "holist" or "wholist", one for whom the false separation of spiritual from material matters or indeed Christian mission from Christian unity, must be rejected, for life in its wholeness is holy before God. His earning of the title of "reconciler" - *muphemaniski* - was thus fully deserved. Many years ago, when the personal and private lives of missionaries were generally concealed from the local community, Stephen came upon two young, quick-tempered Scots in eye-ball to eye-ball confrontation. But he did not slink away. Instead, with a loving hand on the shoulder of each of them, he quietened their hearts and gave them peace. The concept of the church as the Body of Christ was central to his understanding. This therefore was to equip him for a special role in the critical and frightening days in early March 1959.

On the evening of March 2, the Nyasaland Governor, Robert Armitage was reported by radio to have stated that though a State of Emergency had been ordered in Southern Rhodesia and a limited ban had been placed on the Zambia African National Congress in Northern Rhodesia, there would be no Emergency declared in Nyasaland. Shortly before midnight, however, he declared a State of Emergency and swift concerted action by troops of the Central African Federation netted, sometimes violently, hundreds of officials

15

and members of the African National Congress from all parts of the Protectorate. The military called that action "Operation Sunrise", no doubt in cynical response to the country-wide slogan of the ANC: *Kwacha Ngwee* - the dawn has come bright and clear.

On 6 March, a small plane dropped a number of expended tear-gas canisters, each marked confidential and addressed to the Principal of Overtoun Institution, myself. The letter enclosed came from the Provincial Commissioner, and offered safe conduct, under cover of darkness that night, for mission staff to Nkhata Bay.

I called an immediate meeting of the Senatus, the majority of whose members at that time were Malawians. I had made it clear that "confidential" messages to the Principal would be communicated in confidence, by him to the Senatus, as the governing body of the Institution was essentially conciliar. The PC's letter was read and responses called for. All missionaries present declared their intention to remain at Livingstonia. A message to this effect would be sent down the escarpment road to Chitimba and delivered there at 4 am to the master of the vessel, *Ncheni*, which would be lying off the shore to hear our reply. Then Stephen Kauta Msiska, Moderator of the Synod of Livingstonia, asked if he might say something and do so in Tumbuka. What he said was this: "*Mughanaghanenge kuruta, mphanyi tapulikiska. Kweni murutenge, mphanyi thupi la Kristu lasweka.*" ("If you had decided to go, we would have understood. But if you had gone, the body of Christ would have been broken.") At once a deep sense of peace came among us and bound us together more closely than ever before.

The wholeness of Stephen Kauta's life has often brought to my mind a fascinating word for "truth" in the Bemba language of Zambia: *ubufuma-chumi*, meaning literally "the quality from which springs life". For those who believe in Jesus, this notion affirms that truth and love are, as it were, the two sides of the coinage of the kingdom without which we cannot play our part in Christ's commerce with the worlds. Truth without love and love without truth are thus not legal tender in his kingdom. Stephen's blend of gentleness with honesty has consistently demonstrated the essential strength of compassion

16

when life is inspired by the way of Christ who is, at one and the same time, "the power and the wisdom of God" (1 Corinthians 1:24). And this is an affirmation of the fact that those who are reviled and persecuted because of their loyalty to Christ are indeed blessed people (Matthew 5:10-12).

Faith in Tribulation

I believe it is therefore fitting to recount here something which has informed not only Stephen Kauta's thoughts as collated in this book, but the pattern of his daily life and also his prayers profoundly since 1961 and crucially since 1972. For, 35 years ago, the Church of Central Africa Presbyterian came to a clear recognition of his spirituality and his scholarship, when he was sent on a year's study in the Divinity Faculty of Edinburgh University. He visited us in 1961 when I was in parish ministry in Greenock. I sensed then how much he was enjoying the sharpened foci provided by such concentrated study. In 1962 he was appointed to the staff of the united theological college which had recently been established at Nkhoma in the Central Region to serve the three Synods of the CCAP. A few years later he was elevated to the principalship of that college, the first Malawian to be entrusted with such a high degree of responsibility for theological training. I can well imagine the delight which that appointment must have given, no less to his "sweetheart" than to himself.

But the euphoria was to be quickly clouded over by a sharp controversy over the issue of where such a college, created to serve the whole country, should be physically located. Stephen was clear in his own mind that, with the establishment of Chancellor College campus at Zomba in 1972, as part of the University of Malawi, the united theological college should be transferred south to a site within the orbit of what was becoming the national locus of higher education. Though not alone in this opinion, he was immediately confronted by vigorous opposition from both the Synod of Nkhoma (formerly the mission field of the Dutch Reformed Church from South Africa) and the ruling Malawi Congress Party whose power base was in the

17

Central Region. I remember him telling me of the pain he and Nyauzumara had felt when a respected white South African member of staff declined an invitation to a meal at the Principal's house for fear of incurring the disapproval of the headquarters staff of the DRC mission. The fact that the Principal was "non-white" would have offended the "principal" of *apartheid*. On hearing that, I vividly recalled my own brief visit to Nkhoma Mission in 1947, when I discovered that no Africans were allowed within the missionary compound after dark without a permit signed by a white person. *Apartheid* at the heart of an enterprise founded in the name of the Son of God in whom "there is neither Jew nor Greek, bond nor free, male nor female, for you are all one in Christ Jesus" (Galatians 3:28)!

This divisive controversy about the site of the college was still simmering when, in 1974, Stephen Kauta told his students that they should be plainly dressed when conducting worship and should therefore avoid ornamenting themselves. He thus clearly discouraged the wearing of lapel badges with the head of President Banda on them. The reaction to this was swift and fierce with the Malawi Congress Party describing his statement as an act of rebellion. Noisy threats against him and his family were so inflamed that the Kautas had to flee for their lives to their home in the Henga valley. Stephen was personally threatened with death by a senior MCP official and leaders of the CCAP were summoned to hear a warning that such "insolence" on the part of other leaders could lead to the banning of the church.

For the Kautas, this sudden blow was to lead them into a loneliness darkened by fear, for the threats had not been withdrawn. So the high hopes and the exhilaration of his principalship, so rudely extinguished, were inevitably replaced by the experience, as it were, of being in a dungeon. Their faith was therefore sorely tested. Their comfort had to be sought in scripture, like, for example, Paul's words to the church in Corinth (2 Corinthians 1:3-7 and 4:1-12). Without that special quality of love that Stephen and his wife have always shared, their burden of fear, humiliation and ostracism would have been even harder to bear. I believe that this little book will be validated if we find in it some of the fruits of a life lived to God's glory, both "in season" and "out of season" (2 Timothy 4:1-2).

So I hope that, as I am, readers will be grateful to Stephen Kauta for what he is sharing with us here.

In conclusion, let me say how deeply thrilled I have been, on the various return visits I have been able to make to Malawi in recent years, by the spirit of wholehearted adoration and thanksgiving that pervades the weekly worship of huge congregations in packed houses of prayer; worship that is not limp lip-service but an offering of people's whole selves, body, mind and heart.

Fergus Macpherson, formerly Principal, Overtoun Institution
Penpont, Scotland, January 1997

Traditional Religion among the Tumbuka and Other Tribes

Introduction

Throughout the centuries there have been attempts to cut off the religious past as in the time of the second century when the heresiarch Marcion attempted to sever Christianity completely from the Old Testament. When the Christian gospel was first preached, it revolutionized religious attitudes among the people of Malawi. Everything that was being done in connection with religion was suddenly branded as superstition, paganism, and Satanism by most people who came from the West bringing in the gospel of Jesus Christ, simply because of the two different backgrounds of those who brought in the gospel and those to whom the gospel was preached; the participation in the totality of nature and the particularization of the totality of nature would not have compromised.

The African therefore has left his old religion, and rightly so; but he has many other things which were good for him as an African. He has lost his whole religious past and background on which the Christian faith could have flourished through all time. The African has rightly thrown out his dirty, torn old shirt, but he has at the same time lost his golden buttons with it. He is a wise man who can warn his people of what is to happen in the future by remembering what happened in the past and present. Both J.V. Taylor in *The Primal Vision*[1] and Bishop Stephen Neill in *Christian Faith and other Faiths*[2] have said that God was present in Africa and was everywhere revealing himself in a general way to all people, whose return to himself he has been awaiting (cf. Luke 15:11-32). This is the same God who in a unique

---

[1]   J.V. Taylor, *The Primal Vision: Christian Presence Amid African Religion*, London: SCM, 1963.

[2]   S. Neill, *Christian Faith and Other Faiths: The Christian Dialogue with Other Religions*, London: Oxford University Press, 1961.

and special way revealed himself to Israel. "He is the same yesterday, today and tomorrow." For if we were to say that the one supreme God, the Creator, was unknown to the Africans, we can easily contradict ourselves when we come to teach Christian theology of divine initiative. Humanity failed to find God. God himself revealed himself to humanity. He first loved us! If we were to say that the God of the Africans was another God who, in the face of God, the Father of our Lord Jesus Christ, has disappeared, "Who" asked the old man Mr Ndelele, "then looked after the people of Africa?" In other words how can we teach that God is one in three and three in one? Who is the Creator of the *whole* world? Where can we really impress an African on the point of monotheism, if in the past there were continental gods? It is true that the approach to the one God was wrong from the point of view of human beings who were themselves wrong-doers. The Bible tells us that humanity fell away from the Creator.[3] It may be true that the nation of Malawi did not really understand about this one supreme God, but the fact remains that they still worshipped their Creator in a dim way. Thank God that it has become clear in his Son Jesus Christ: "He, who has seen me, has seen the Father" (John 14:9). God is emphatically and truly one.

The Alternative: Backward or Forward?

The consequence of this misunderstanding has been that in Malawi people have left their old religion, this being a step that was required of them in order for them to receive Christ the Lord - but they have only touched Christianity on the surface and have never become real Christians. They have not received Christ as their Saviour and their Lord in everything, because when they are confronted with temptations, pain and death, they tend to go back to their old religious ways. They have become religiously indifferent, which is dangerous in any country. This means that the influence of their old religion is ever

---

[3]   Genesis 3; cf. T. Cullen Young, *African Ways and Wisdom*, London: United Society for Christian Literature, 1937.

with them, noticeable whenever and wherever people are in trouble, pain, disappointment and death.

People tend to go back, but in fact they have lost the way to do so. Instead, there happens a further tragedy, namely the mixing up of religions or a syncretism of the old religion, Christianity and Islam.

There was a man in the northern region of this country called Chikanga who, from 1957-65, claimed to be a prophet and a healer. He claimed to reveal all secret causes of trouble and death. Many people came to him from Tanzania, Zambia, Mozambique, as well as from within Malawi. People came to hear about their troubles and find out the witchcraft and witches in their homes. In the ceremonies there, he and his followers sang Christian hymns and rendered Christian prayers as well as divining and marking the faces of people. He claimed to have received this power from God in order to remove all witchcraft, before people received political freedom and peace. Before his time, there was a group of people from the southern region known as *Mchape*; who went throughout the whole country removing *ufiti* (witchcraft). They operated by gathering people in a village on the authority of the chief. The whole gathering sat in a large circle and one *Mchape* danced inside with a mirror in his hand. Most of the songs they sang were Christian hymns adapted to simple village tunes. They claimed to have received the power direct from God.

When Bishop Lesslie Newbigin visited the area in 1958, at a Bible study group one young man burst out during a silence and said: "We must go back to our ancestors' worship where our God heard us and answered our prayers. We are now in trouble because we worship the western God." But the proper meaning of "going back" was not clear in this young man's mind. He did not remember the punishment for sinners, which was burning or torturing and death. There is a place in the north called Jochero where sinners were burned. He did not remember the many rules and customs involved in that religion. There is no going back. The only healthy position is to go forward and keep the best of our own customs and not merely to copy other people's without good cause. To go forward and to become true Christians, accepting Christ as our Saviour and Lord.

The other indication of the indifferent attitude of most nominal Christians in the country can be observed clearly in regard to their way of worship. Worship to them is without rules, laws, customs, taboos or restrictions; worship and morality are two different things. They seem to think that it does not matter what one does in private from Monday to Saturday. They feel that they are now free in the Christian church, like the New Testament Nicolaitans and Antinomians. Sunday is not a holy day but a social day, the gentleman's day for showing off his suit and new car. This is the day to meet friends.

If one stopped here, it would be for reasons of pride. There are some fine Christians in Malawi and there have been wise European Christian leaders throughout the history of the church of Christ in the country.

In this introduction, I should also inform readers of the difficulties of research. Whenever one asks an old man about the old religions, one is bound to detect a great deal of Christianity which has crept in. Christianity has influenced even the minds of those who have never been in the church.

Religion before European Contact

It is a most striking point to notice that Africa is a vast continent; and among the Bantu, though there are differences, yet there are many things which are alike, mostly in connection with their conception of God. The Bantu seem to have come from the same place and the same forefathers, long, long ago.[4] In the north of Malawi (Karonga), there are the Nkonde who claim to have come from or through Uganda; and the first chief "Kyungu" Gwazapasi seems to have first settled in Karonga in the second half of the 11th century, bringing with him his religion—which in many respects is not so very different

---

[4]   T.R. Batten: *Africa Past and Present,* London: African Welfare Series, 1943.

from the Tumbuka, Chewa and Asenga of the central and southern regions. The Tumbuka came from the north probably in the same century as the Nkonde and scattered through Zambia, Tanzania and Malawi on their way down the continent.

The Tumbuka-Balowoka,[5] who settled round about part of Karonga, Rumphi and the whole of West Nyasa (Bandawe, etc.), settled in the country before the arrival of the Ngoni, in the beginning of the 19th century. These Tumbuka crossed the Lake from the east. The Chewa came from or through Zambia. You can observe the matrilineal system of marriage as one of the obvious evidences of this; the Chewa and their brothers the Asenga came together. So there are the Nkonde, the Chewa, the Tumbuka the Yao, and the Ngoni. These can be divided into many sub-divisions.

Now, the point is that among the people mentioned above there is a slight difference in their conception of God. They all worshipped God through their ancestors' spirits, and higher spirits. They all offered sacrifices, they all had ritual observances, they all had *basofi* (priests, soothsayers); they all prayed for rain, success and health. They all had the same set responsive prayers, all hymns, nearly all had the same restrictions and customs and taboos. But they entered this country of Malawi from different directions: Nkonde from the north through Tanzania, Tumbuka from the north through Zambia and Tanzania, east of Lake Nyasa, and the Chewa and Senga from the west through Zambia. The Yao came from the south, and may be different from the others because of their early contact with the Arabs.

The Creator, higher spirits and ancestors

As shown in the diagram on p. 25, all cults or religions in Malawi were based on the belief in one God.[6] In the north of the country he was

---

5   See Cullen Young, *African Ways and Wisdom*.

6   Cf. E.G. Parrinder: *African Traditional Religion,* 2nd ed., London: SPCK, 1962, pp. 43-54.

Chiuta, Kyala, Mbanda or *Mbepomwikemo* (God-spirit-wind) among the Tumbuka and Nkonde people. He is *Chauta, Mulungu, Chisumphi, Mphambi, Leza, Nduna*, among the mixed tribes of the Achewa and Ngoni in the central region (the Ngoni who conquered the people in Malawi after crossing the Zambezi had themselves been conquered by the language and the religion of the country). He is *Leza, Mulungu, Mulengi, Chauta* in the southern regions. All three regions in the country agree in calling God *Mulungu* or *Mulengi*, (creator); *Chiuta* or *Chauta* which probably meant the greatest power above all powers, unseen, almighty, omnipresent and highly personified; the King of kings. *Uta* in all three languages means "bow". The root meaning of Chauta or Chiuta is the same everywhere. *Chi* always shows size or quality; such as *chimunthu* which means "a big or ugly man", *chilolo* which means "prime minister" or "advisor". If the "bow" is small, it is *kauta*; if it is medium, it is *uta*: but if it is extraordinarily large, as the sign of power it is *chiuta* or *chauta*. The name of *Leza*[7] comes from the word *M'leza*, "one who looks after the little ones". Kulela has the same meaning, "to feed the little ones". Leza is "he who looks after children".

People in Malawi did not worship their ancestors' spirits, but they worshipped *through* them. One notices how strange this point may sound to those who have read many books by anthropologists who have insisted on ancestor worship, but the fact remains that even among the most ignorant people of Malawi this is inconceivable to them. If this had not been so, Christianity would have had no meaning at all to a people for whom there was no preparation for or revelation of God. There was some knowledge of the one Creator God who was unapproachable, too high for human beings down on earth, and too high even for those who had died. Therefore approach to Chauta or Chiuta was conceived by people on earth as being possible only through the ranks of those who had gone nearer to him after death. Men on earth could therefore speak to him in prayers and worship through their own ancestors who were nearer him. Each

---

[7]   E.W. Smith, *The Secret of the African*, London: SCM, 1929.

tribe, each clan, each household could worship God through a well-known relative who understood their needs. No one could approach the chief in a village without first going to his messenger; the messenger then went to the counselor, who then consulted the chief on behalf of the man in need. It may be that the chief would see the man personally, but it was always by the will of the chief and not the suppliant. No son or daughter would directly consult their father without first consulting their mother about their problems, whether fees, pocket money, school or other things. This was a great honour to the chief or the father. So how much more to the Creator!

The change came when missionaries said that they had brought the true God and our fathers deduced that the strange God they brought was the true God. They ought to have said that the God for whom people had been searching in different ways and in different places has himself come down and is among them *through* his Son, Jesus Christ. The God whom people by their own knowledge and wisdom cannot find has revealed himself through his Son, who is Emmanuel, "God with his people." It seems that Chiuta or Chauta then deserted his people in Malawi, and now people are trying to find this lost God who was their own God, who sympathized with them in all their needs. People now are confused in their religious life. God has always been thought of as *one*. There was once an old village headman named Chibaya near Livingstonia who died in 1929. In his old age he was converted and came to be examined by Dr Laws in 1914. The missionary asked the first question: "Well, Chibaya, how many Gods are there in the universe?" Chibaya answered: "*Dotolo* (Doctor), are you losing your head? The God who created you and me and all people *is* only one God." Dr Laws replied: "Well, Chibaya, you have answered very well. Go and be baptized and God bless you." Monotheistic belief seems to have been traditional in Malawi as in other countries of Africa. But the approach to this God was not right; the people of Malawi as well as all other people in the world, all mankind, lost their way to their Creator, until "in the fulness of time God sent forth his own Son..." In each area, there were *basofi*, priests or leaders of worship. In all three regions in Malawi these important men were found who were often chiefs themselves. They were given

26

food and other necessities of life; they were not supposed to become drunk; they had to live exemplary lives as well as caring for their people spiritually. Each *musofi* worshipped God through their ancestors' spirits mentioned by name, who would then appeal to higher spirits nearer God himself.

The higher spirits were earlier *basofi*, or chiefs who had been leaders of exemplary life, men of authority and good reputation. Known now by the Tumbuka name *vipiri*, and in the central and southern regions they were called *agogo* (sing. *gogo* and in Tumbuka, *chipiri*), their spirits now spoke with and remained in communion with God. See the following:

1. The high God (Chauta, Chiuta, Mulungu or Mulengi, Leza).
2. The higher spirits (vipiri, agogo).
3. The ancestors' spirits (mizimu).
4. The priests or leaders (basofi).
5. The people on earth (hantu).
6. Under the earth, the dwelling place of the dead (malo gha bakufwa).

(Nos 2-4 are good or important chiefs or priests. Only the good ones are here.)

The overall system of the supernatural

As shown above, we therefore have the following system: (a) People living on earth, revealing their needs to the *basofi*; (b) the *basofi* who convey these needs to the ancestors' spirits, the *mizimu*; (c) the *mizimu* forward these needs to the higher spirits, the *vipiri*; and (d) the *vipiri* or *agogo* convey these needs to God (Chiuta, Mulungu or Chauta); (e) so at the top is God, who answered his people's prayers by giving them rain, food, children, health, success in war, happiness, freedom and peace, when approached through this series of stages.

Each of these five levels was distinct. Within a level, there were relationships, thus the higher spirits would visit each other, and the *mizimu* likewise. There was even marriage between the *vipiri*; for

27

example, Chombe had his wife down on the lake-shore who was known as Chombe-Mwanakazi, the female Chombe. When the husband moved to his wife there was a heavy storm as a sign of this journey. There was also fighting among the *vipiri*, as for example Chikhan'gombe fighting Chombe because Chombe's people killed one of the Chikhang'ombes while searching for food. The signs of this struggle were heavy storms, thunder and lightening at unlikely times outside the rainy season. Sometimes Chombe wanted to send rain, but Chikhang'ombe would cause a great wind to drive away the rains. Each was responsible for a certain area, clan or tribe. The whole web of relationship was derived from these origins. In the northern region lived the *vipiri*, and attached to them were the *nchimi*, the soothsayers, those who could foretell the future. These *nchimi* were in most places women, and in the central region were more often girls. They usually prophesied when in an ecstatic mood, and people acted at once at their word.

Regions and regional spirits

The following is a list of several of the major areas in Malawi with their own local spirits (the first of the two names is that of the higher spirit, the second of the *musofi*). Beginning from the north:

1. *Karonga*
   (a) Filawule - Kilambo and his family
   (b) Chisindile - Mwenechisindile
   (c) Kwa Chimbwe - Mwenelubale
   (d) Kwa Mphande - Kalambo
   (e) Lupembe - Mwenelupembe.
2. *Fulirwa*: Wovo or Furu - Kanyuka Mwafulirwa.
3. *Deep Bay* (now Chilumba): Chitende - Mponera.
4. *Khondowe* (Livingstonia): Manchebe (2 miles from Livingstonia): Manchebe - Mwabanga Msiska.
5. *Chombe*: Chombe - with three basofi: Chibiribiri Haraba, Khulakula Msowoya, and Mwachipoka.

6. *Mlowe*: Wongwe - Msofi Mvula (the name *musofi* or *msofi* has here become a proper name for the leader of worship, similar to the name "minister" or "priest").
7. *Henga*: Phwezi - Tundulu Mhango.
8. *Mhuju*: Jerekere - Kangu Nyirongo.
9. *Uzumara*: Munguyi - Khalikali Mzumara.
10. *Ng'onga*: Kampaba - Chavwaya Mkandawire.
11. *Hebe*:
    (a) Mwanda - Mlomboji Mkandawire.
    (b) Chikhang'ombe - Mwachanda Mkandawire.
12. *Nkhoma*: Nkhoma - Mazengera (the latter's great grandson is now Native Authority in this area).
13. *Emanyaleni*: Kuzubahenga - Kumwenda.
14. *Chawuwa* (about 10 miles from Nkhoma): Chawuwa - Chawuwa.

Regular days of worship

There seem to have been in traditional religion no regular days of worship as such, but there were resting days which were appointed by the *musofi*. These were in connection with harvest festivals, and the day of atonement, when all brought different gifts to the ancestors' spirits. Usually this day would be appointed during trouble or war, famine or disease. All came together on the atonement day to confess their sins in prayer. The *musofi* would stand up, and each man came forward confessing his sins or declaring his innocence. The *musofi* in a short confessional prayer would say: "O God, thou art omniscient and knowest the hearts of thy people." The response would be: "Away! Away! Sweep the hidden sins away! Blow these sins away!"

The *musofi* then prayed: "O God, grant us thy pardon." The response: "We thank Thee." The *musofi*: "Let thy people not hide their sins." Response: "Blow away all the sins!" This response in the Tumbuka language is *Fya*, a word used everywhere one chases birds away from rice fields: *Fya!* "Away!" But this prayer would be considered incomplete if it only mentioned God, and so the *musofi* begins by mentioning one after the other the names of departed ancestors. Reference is also made to relatives left here on earth. "Mr. Chibiribiri, have you forgotten Chidongo, Kasiwa?" etc. At this point all listeners become as quiet as mice. Hence the *musofi* had to be a man who knew everybody in the area in which he was working. Sometimes the response was by clapping of hands. For example at Karonga the *musofi* would say, mentioning the names of those on earth to *filawule:* "Speak for us to *Kyala* (God) who is *Mbamba* (one God), *Kayuwili* (who knows everything), *Mwalankusa* (who is all times)". Then there was clapping of hands.

Regular days of worship were as follows: (1) At the time of the rains; (2) at the time of harvest; (3) in time of trouble; (4) at the new moon. At any new moon, prayer would be offered by all praying for unborn children, boys or girls. *"Kamuperekezeni, mutipeko mwana msepuka."* - "You bright light, give us a baby-boy." (5) At the birth of a child, a short prayer would be offered first by important old women; and after the umbilical cord is broken, by the important men in the village who would come one by one and say: *"Kahedi"* (welcome to this world) *"Chiuta pera"* (literally, "all is from God"). "This is a gift which is direct from thee, O God, we have done nothing towards it." This has remained even in our time, in the saying: *"Yewo, Chiuta pera."* - "Thank you, let us trust in God."

When people listened to the harangue or preaching on such occasions, there was dead silence. They would then be told in detail what to do and how to behave. Time was not worrying them because although Africans then had some ideas about time, it did not rule them as it does now.

In time of drought, men, women and children would gather together bringing a goat with many other gifts. The goat was killed and the liver cooked in a special clean new pot (such as in the central region). All went to *kavuba*, a tiny house built for worship. The *musofi* placed a pot of cooked liver into *karuwa* with this prayer: "O God, we are dying, there is no rain." Response: *"Phepa"* (Excuse us). The *musofi:* "Hear us we pray to thee. Your children die" - *"Phepa"*. After the

30

prayer was over and the sacrifice of cooked liver put into *karuwa*, all with cheerful heart began to sing and dance. They were certain rain would then immediately fall: every old man and woman I consulted in this investigation affirmed that rain always then came immediately; before they could reach home, they were always soaked to the skin in the rain.

Hymns and songs were antiphonal and responsive, and always took the form of prayers for different occasions. For rains in the north: *"Jimutambo"* (sky), to which the people answered: *"Lira-lira"* (cry aloud), *"nkayiguza nkayibika apa"* (I pulled it and put it here, whatever is given me). In other words: Please open the skies so that rain falls like tears, and we shall have maize to eat and enjoy." In the central region the song would be like this: *"Vura pano! Siyikugwa, kokwe!"* Response: *"Kalole! Kalole! Kalole!"* - "Here we have no rain, send it down please." Response: "It will be wonderful! wonderful! wonderful! wonderful!"

If a song was to call one of the higher spirits to eat what was offered in sacrifice, the words were: *"Mwize! Mwize! Inu a pamwamba."* Response: *"Mudye! Mudye! Mudye za ana anu!"* - "Come! Come! Come! you higher spirits!" Response: "And eat! Eat! Eat! what has been offered to you by your own children". If in a village, hunters have been successful in hunting and they have killed a large animal, the singing would be: *"Apo pali nyama, apo pali nyama, para nyama yinye muyireke yirye utheka yitetemere. Pa sirya pali bachibanda, bachibanda ndikomerani nyama ndiryepo."* - "There is an animal (three times). There is a hunter, kill it for me." These words are a prayer because they are sung and said by the hunter himself on seeing an animal, and are sung by all after the animal has been killed. Then all gather round a big fire with meat on top of the fire being roasted, and the hunter himself dances while all clap their hands. There are hymns sung while the people go up to the high places for worship, as well as hymns of joy when they return from them. All these hymns would be sung with attendant drumming and dancing.

In traditional religion, sacrifices were of three kinds: (a) Sacrifices for the propitiation of ancestors' spirits because people on earth had

31

offended them by breaking a law or custom and had caused the innocent to suffer throughout the area. Hence the sacrifice was made on behalf of all people living in that area. (b) Sacrifices offered for some particular need, such as success in war, the well-being of the clan or tribe, a large catch of fish on the lake, or for success in hunting. An individual could offer on his own this kind of sacrifices. (c) Sacrifices offered before crossing a dangerous river or climbing a hill, or passing through holy or dangerous places. One sometimes notices the remains of this when one climbs a hill and finds a large heap of stones. One can also hear many stories of Njakwa bridge which people would not cross until having thrown a white fowl, beads or food into the water. Signs of acceptance of the sacrifice were then sought in movements of currents on the surface of the water.

Sacrifices consisted of goats, cattle, fowls, beads and food, both cooked and uncooked. Animals had to be the best ones with no blemish. They had to be of only one colour, preferably white or black. They had to be big and fat. In regard to food, each person in a clan or tribe had to give something. A little would be left at the place of worship, and the rest would be eaten by the *musofi*, the priest himself. If the sacrifice was offered for the troubles people faced, the victim would be burned into ashes on the altar of the new fire; this sacrifice was offered direct to God and therefore nobody took a share of it at all. All the chiefs present then took fire from there for their villages.[8]

Worship was centred on certain places: under large trees, near mountains, rivers, waterfalls, huge stones or in caves. A famous place in the south of Malawi was Mulanje Mountain, the highest in the country and over nine thousand feet high. To most people living around, it is a holy place evoking awe and foreboding. A few other holy places are: Zomba, Dedza, Chawuwa, Nkhoma, Mwanda, Chikhang'ombe, Nkonjera, Usowoya, Uzumara, Chombe, Njakwa and Filawule.

---

[8]   Parrinder, *African Traditional Religion,* p. 88.

Throughout the country, on an appointed holy day, people would gather with gifts ready to offer. They would then be organized by the *musofi* with his helpers into single file and complete silence would fall. The *musofi* spoke on their behalf, first praising all ancestral spirits. Then prayer was offered: *"Tipatseni madzi kukhosi kwa uma"* - "Give us water for we are thirsty." *"Kokwe, kalole!"* the people's response: *"Fya"* would then be accompanied by singing and dancing with drums, all of which served to arouse the emotions of the audience. Quietness and silence before the holy place were regarded as great virtues, signifying humility. Each gift was then offered to ancestral spirits mentioned by name: "We offer this for Mr So-and So", etc.

At a certain place in the north called Katenku, there was a hole in the rock where people offered beer to the spirits by taking a cup and saying: "This is for you, Mr So-and-So", "This is for you Mrs So-and-So; we give this not to satisfy you, but to show our own need and our own troubles."[9] If, after all the names had been mentioned, the hole was not yet filled, the *musofi* would say: "Ah! remember that your children would like to enjoy what is left over." The whole was then filled, and what was left over was shared by all who came for worship, children as well as adults. Cattle were also brought and killed, and a portion left in the small hut *kavuba* or *kachisi*; the remainder was divided amongst those present to take home. Finally all would stand up, shouting, singing and dancing, and would return home with great joy. But there was a strict prohibition: no one could look back or remove anything from the *kachisi*. And as they returned they took with them the new fire kindled there.

Penalties for offending the spirits

A story is told of one who went back to take a bigger share in the meat left at *kachisi*. He found on arrival that all the dead were there and that the meat had become multiplied. When he appeared the dead said: "Come, do not be afraid, we know you want meat; here

---

[9]   *Ibid*, p. 87.

you are, take it, but do not tell anybody at home." The man was excited at having seen his own dead father alive. He returned home and gave his wife the meat with great joy. But since he kept on clapping his hands and expressing his wonder aloud, his wife insisted on knowing what had happened. The man did not say a word; later on he told his wife what had actually happened, then he fell down dead.

Spirits could sometimes be angry with people on earth because they had not kept certain rules and regulations; perhaps someone had committed adultery, or had sexual intercourse with his wife before she had finished her menstruation period, or had not cared for orphans left by his brother, Or perhaps they had eaten food from the gardens before the spirits had a taste. The signs of their anger would then be shown either by failure and defeat in war, by a lion killing people in villages, or by failure of the harvest or drought. Sometimes it was due to direct provocation of specific spirits.

At Mphizi, on the lakeshore near Livingstonia, a story is told of two girls who were missing. What happened was that while people were hoeing and drinking beer, a snake slowly pushed its head through the pot for a drink. When people saw this they attempted to kill it, but it escaped. Immediately after, two girls disappeared; one of them, Nyankombole, subsequently died in 1952 in her old age. They were lost a long time until the old moon set. The *nchimi* (soothsayer) stood up and told the people where the girls were and why they were missing. Two white fowls and some brewed beer were offered. The two girls reappeared but were unable to hear for some time. They had been, so they said, underneath in the earth where they saw the dead alive. The girls told a story of another soothsayer under the earth who was able to tell the people of the mistakes one of them made in the form of a snake. The dead person could appear to people in different forms, sometimes in the form of a snake, or a bird like the giant ground horn-bill, or others. The snake that drank beer was one of such men from the underworld.

These departed spirits, both men and women, are able to eat; they can also speak in language unintelligible to those on earth. They are capable of seeing us here, but we do not see them nor can we. If they are discussing someone who is passing by, perhaps a grandson or a grand-daughter, they can make him turn his face to them by breaking a dried twig or by throwing a stone. So the man turns round, and so they see him.

Only those who were good men and women are in that underworld, as an old lady, Sarah by name, told me; the bad ones wander about everywhere and their destroying spirits can be diverted by bad men on earth through magic and *ufiti* to kill others. The spirits of bad men are not at peace there and because of them there is pain and suffering on earth. The man who is clearly known to be a bad one, at his death, is buried with charcoals as a sign of excommunication from any intercommunication with the living.

The discipline of traditional religion

All bad men and women, thieves, adulterers, witches, liars were tortured, killed or burned alive. There is a place near Livingstonia called Jochero (incinerator), where they used to burn people until recently.[10] Only in 1890-1900 with the arrival of the gospel of Christ was this stopped. You can still see charcoals and broken bits of pots. This was done at one place and in public. Obedience was inevitable and enforced through fear. One should not criticise this method since it was suitable at the time.

The Place of Christ in Traditional Religion

Earlier in this article we mentioned the different people who came to this country by different routes and settled down. But their settlement was disturbed by the coming of two different peoples. The first were the Arab half-castes buying slaves from Mwaya down to Nkhotakota. And the second were the Ngoni of Zulu origin from South Africa, who came from South Africa through the colossal operation of

---

[10]   W.P. Livingstone, *Laws of Livingstonia*, London: Hodder & Stoughton, n.d., p. 121.

Tshaka, whose career of wholesale massacre shook Southern Africa to its foundation in the beginning of the 19th century. They crossed the Zambezi and entered Malawi; they raided the weak tribes and plundered their food and cattle, though they were conquered by their victims in language and religion. Then the Tumbuka and the Chewa moved away from their villages and gardens, and hid themselves in the mountains, in their sacred places.

The new that came with Christ

Then in the second half of the 19th century the gospel of our Lord Jesus Christ was brought by the servants of Christ, "For the tender compassion of our God, the morning sun from heaven, will rise upon us, to shine on those who live in darkness, under the cloud of death, and to guide our feet into the way of peace" (Luke 1:78-9).

One is inclined to think that the gospel of our Lord Jesus Christ should first of all concentrate on the unity of the Godhead without being tied down by the historical Christological controversy of the 4th century raised by Arius. We must present the gospel first and foremost with emphasis on the unity of God who created the universe, who did come down to be with his people in his Son Jesus Christ, who, being divine and human, was able to reconcile God and humanity for our salvation. He remains amongst his people in the power of the Holy Spirit to lead them and teach them "all things" unto salvation from taboos, torture, fire and customs. He is the God who by revealing himself to man has conquered sin and death on the cross. He is the Father of our Lord Jesus Christ and is near at hand; he is in our hearts and we can live in immediate communion with him. Jesus Christ is not just the greatest of our *vipiri* or higher spirits; but he is God among men. He has come to live among us, and the whole hierarchy of our ancestors has lost its traditional meaning; this is to say that in Jesus Christ we have no need for any other intermediary between God and us. He is all that we need for our fellowship with him. This is what is new in the message of Christ.

36

What are the golden buttons an African has lost?

(a) An African has been disturbed in his belief in one God not through the method of presenting the gospel to him by a missionary, but because some missionaries interpreted the gospel with too strong an emphasis on their own cultural background. In some missionary theology, the God who revealed himself in a general way to all people, and was approached in wrong ways by people of this country namely through their ancestors spirits, was called *remote* and an idol.

(b) The way of praying is lost. In most of our Christian churches, only one man speaks to God in prayer and others are merely spectators; the result is that most of the audience sleep. There is no participation and response to prayer.

(c) There is lack of humiliation and silence. There is no respect paid to our older people, and it is therefore more difficult to have humility before God. Observing how other people behave in services, Africans wrongly imitate them: you will find people talking to each other in the church.

(d) There was a spirit in the traditional religion which seems to be disappearing in our modern time.

(e) If in traditional religion through fear men and women lived a good life, it is through the love of God that we should be living better lives, but instead religion and morality have been separated.

(f) African singing was accompanied by drums and other instruments to keep its rhythm and arouse emotional feelings, an important element in any religion. Singing freely, rhythm and clapping of hands with graceful movements of the body are lost.

"As long as Christianity is presented to the people in European terms, under European forms, it must remain an exotic faith to them. It may gain a certain prestige as of a powerful race but sooner or later their national spirit rises and they revolt against the domination of an alien culture which has been imposed in one way or another. They come to see that they too are a people, and they will cherish resentment against all who conspired to rob them of their heritage. Unless by that time Christianity has become deeply rooted in their souls they will turn from it as a foreign and therefore a hateful institution. And it will never be so rooted unless it be presented to them in the terms of their own thought and expressed in their own speech."[11]

These then, are some of the traditional ways in Malawi. Countless nominal Christians hanker after aspects of them and hover between them on the one hand and orthodox mission Christianity on the other. The problem is what can be done about it, and to what extent, if at all, the new religion can be related to the old in order to lead people to a Christian faith they can whole-heartedly accept?

[11]   E.W. Smith, *The Shrine of a People's Soul,* London: Edinburgh House Press, 1929, p. 45.

The Certainty of Christianity among the People in the Villages

I am not a scientist, a theologian or a philosopher. I am just a simple and common man who for many years has been teaching in CCAP Theological Schools. I now live in a society which is a mixed one - Christians and non-Christians. I have been interested to find out real distinctions between them, which as yet I cannot. I am not saying that they are both bad or good, no, but that one cannot find any distinction of any kind except on Sundays when those who are baptised go to church for worship. But in burying the dead or in community engagements, or in marriage celebrations and dancing, even where the witchdoctors gather up people to search them, the majority of Christians are present. Subjects for conversation and discussions are nearly the same. For according to our environment, there is nothing wrong with these public activities. It may be that we need to examine ourselves and see whether Christianity has some things which ought to be separated from our common historical background.

We take it for granted that in Christianity we believe in God, the Father, Almighty Creator, the Father of our Lord Jesus Christ. We claim that it is our Lord Jesus Christ who has revealed God as Father through the power of the Holy Spirit. This is the Christian God whom we worship. If we ask ourselves the difficult question: "What is Christianity?", one would give a general answer - Christianity is Christ, who is both the Founder and the Foundation. What happens then, when someone becomes a Christian? Paul says that he becomes a new creature. In which way does one become new? Surely, not through his bodily appearance, not even his voice, but his whole outlook of his life. He now knows Christ and Christ's way of life and love, and automatically makes decisions to follow Christ, and do his will. Therefore in Christianity there are things which do not fit in our general behaviour. Things are bound to show that a Christian has become a "new creature", things which do not fit in our customs, culture and habits, things which may separate us from brothers and

39

sisters, mothers and fathers, indeed from our ancestors. What are they?

Christianity to many of us has widened the relationship between human beings based upon the Fatherhood of God taught by Jesus. It has given us freedom and peace. It has bestowed upon us the love of God towards man. It has taught us to love God, others and self truly and honestly. I have now brothers and sisters not only in Africa, but also in Britain, America, and Asia. It is a relationship which does not depend on blood and colour. It has taught us to think and care for other people, help those who are unable to help themselves. It has made us free from the bondage of self-centredness and pride. It has comforted us by solving the problems of pain and death, and directed us to the real life here and hereafter - through him who conquered sin and death for us all. In him death is left behind and therefore fear itself is banished for ever. True happiness and joy, freedom and peace, knowledge and wisdom, strength and power, faith and hope come from him and him alone, Jesus Christ our Lord. In him who is "the Way, the Truth and the Life," we have come to know what we are in Him and that now we can speak our minds and be true to ourselves as well as to God.

In other words Christianity has brought into the world the greatest fellowship which the world had never known before. Its fruits, as Paul expresses it, are: love, joy, peace, patience, kindness, goodness, faithfulness, gentleness and self-control. Slavery is abolished, taboos which made children suffer are moderated; degradation of women is over, segregation and colour bar are highly questioned and discouraged, fear of the unknown is overcome. This we have through Christ.

Christianity and Fear

A word can sometimes be very misleading. Such a word is "fear". We are familiar with the Old Testament text which says, "The fear of the Lord is the beginning of wisdom." The word fear in this case may involve honour, worship, glorification and our complete obedience to our Creator. In our language we use the word in a different sense when we say: "*Ungopanga mphepo iyo yilive kumanya kuthenya nkhuni*". (Do not fear the cold for it cannot collect firewood.) In the New Testament teaching, Christ warns the disciples to fear him who kills the soul. Such is wholesome and necessary for God is the Holy Father and persistent defiance of his will must be visited with stern and righteous doom. When a child is afraid to hurt its father's heart, that child will grow wise and strong, rather than a child who fears beating.

But in our society we do fear the unknown. We fear our ancestors' spirits because they are gathered into an unknown place where we all go after this life; and from where the present control and care for our health and happiness comes. We fear death for it destroys our joys and our life; we fear men and women who are witches for they destroy our existence; we fear to speak our mind for we shall be imprisoned and suffer; we fear those who are above us for they shall put us into trouble; we fear men and women whom we do not know, we fear to speak in meetings because we shall be criticised; we fear to criticise others because we too do exactly the same as they do; we fear those who stand on our way of life because we feel that they are our enemies; we fear darkness because we cannot see and therefore we are in danger of enemies, snakes and harmful animals; we fear to pass by the graveyard by night because the spirits of the dead may harm us; sometimes we fear to pass by because we do not want to be reminded of the faces of our dear ones who are buried there.

We fear Satan because, as many people think, he is continuously fighting against our God, struggling to enslave men and women who are God's creatures. He, Satan, is responsible for every single evil action done by us. He is responsible for wars and squabbles, tensions, conflicts, ruthlessness and guile. He is there to confuse things and make us blind and ignorant, cheating every one of us to regard ourselves as higher, wiser and better than others. What he gives to man at first tastes like honey for a short time, but bitter later on. We fear to do evil in the open, because other people may catch us and we shall be ashamed of it - not because we hate evil as such, but because we fear people. Above all, we fear to speak the truth

41

because very often to speak the truth is to get into trouble as far as the world is concerned.

Now if the reader can examine all these fears above, is he or she in a position to say that all these fears fit into Christianity? We all know that Christianity deals with reality and the exact nature of things. One may be misunderstood here. I am not saying that Christianity must be different from the good world which God created for every one of us. Neither do I wish to make a separation between Christian people and non-Christians. We live and must live together and help each other to learn of Christ and be influenced by Him through men and women who have determined to know Christ and love him. But if Christ makes us free, why should we have manifold fears and doubts in our hearts? If you are travelling in a good and strong car, driven by the most experienced and trusted driver, why should you fear accidents which have never happened? If Christ who conquered sin and death is our hero, why should we have fears of sin and death?

If I read my New Testament rightly, I see that Jesus exhorts his hearers not to fear: Mark 5:36; Luke 8:50; Luke 5:10; Matthew 17:7. In other passages Jesus is against fear: Matthew 10:24-27; Matthew 10:28; Luke 12:4; Matthew 10:31; Luke 12:32. He teaches moral courage: Revelation 21:8; Luke 21:19; Matthew 10:22, 24:13; Luke 12:8; Matthew 10:32. What his disciples saw in him: John 7:26; Matthew 22:16; Matthew 15:1-4; Mark 7:1-13; Matthew 23:1-39. Jesus exhorts his disciples to fear God: Luke 1:50; Luke 18:2, 23:40. On the whole, when we examine the teaching of Jesus on the subject of fear, we see that he constantly urges people to have faith rather than to fear, and to trust in God's fatherly goodness. We know that there is a severity of God which cannot be ignored

As we read in the gospel of John: "If you continue in my word," said Jesus, "you are truly my disciples, and you will know the truth, and the truth will make you free." (John 8:32) So freedom comes from the word of Jesus in which we learn and know the truth which is the source of our freedom. Freedom from fear and anxiety; freedom from self itself (*ego*), freedom from death; freedom of the mind, freedom of speech and expression; freedom of action; freedom to love and freedom to hate; freedom to do and to abstain from doing anything; freedom to choose; freedom of worship. Here and here alone lies our personality, if I would be allowed to say so. Christ likes us to be free in doing what is right and good. If freedom allows us to do anything at all against righteousness to gratify our own ambition, serving only ourselves, then we become the slave of a slave, the slave of oneself. I ought to be free in my own conscience to fulfil the demand of my Lord and my God. If we have faith in Christ, it does not come from the fear of hell and hell-fire. It must come from him who lays down his life for the sake of love for you and for me, so that we may have life, and have it abundantly

Let us take specific examples of fear in our villages and see if they fit into Christianity. On one or two of the funeral services, one was shocked to see that two men went down into the grave with the body of a woman who was pregnant. I fail to write exactly what happened because it was terrifying indeed. The two men with their knife cut the abdominal part of the dead body open, and left it thus. The two men came out and the grave was covered with clay. But why? Well, many reasons are given for it. The one who does the cutting is the husband or his nearest relative. The reason being that the corpse has been known to have the spirits of two human beings, therefore the baby's spirit should not be closed in the womb of its mother. If this is not done, the widower is bound to get into trouble. He may not have any more children at all. This is the fear!

At all burials, one notices that the white cloth, in which the body is wrapped, must have a hole cut in it, opposite the ear. The fear is that if this is not done, the dead will not hear those relatives who are left on earth. The relatives are to speak to their dear ones who have departed when they are in trouble or sorrow or pain. If a man dies who was impotent, who has never left a child here on earth, at his burial he will be marked with charcoal on his back. The mark is like the mark of a cross. There is fear that this man must go for good because he has no one to attract him back to earth to visit his relatives in dreams. If such a man comes back, he will be jealous of other people's families and cause death among them. He will be counted as one of bad spirits which are dangerous to the welfare of

43

the people on earth. The charcoal is black and it is believed that it will close the door.

In our society there are various burials. If a small child dies, the grave must not be dug deep. The fear is that if the mother of the dead child is still young, she will not have any more children. Also if a woman has miscarried or given birth to a still-born baby, the body is put into the grave, but the face is exposed to the light. This is why dogs take the bodies away. If the body of the still-born baby is covered in a proper grave, it is believed that its mother will have no more children at all. So, out of fear, the body of a still-born baby is exposed to the light in order that the mother should continue bearing children. In other communities the bodies are burned to ashes. No respect is given to these burials! The reader may be interested to ask, "Are these people Christians who do these things?" The answer is emphatically "yes".

One knows that such fears are found among many nations in the world, both among Christians and non-christians. I am not accusing them, but the point is: do these fears fit with Christianity? Where is Christian freedom? In other words, from which things does Christ make us free? We must take care when we try answer this question. The question must be answered in word and action, in everyday living. The answer must show itself throughout the whole of life.

I believe that God's will is to have men and women who are free. Human free will is what gives humanity royal dignity and constitutes the innermost secret of having been made in the image of God. That is probably why there is the possibility of rebellion on the part of human beings. God makes human beings free, able to choose good or evil. We, of our own choice, become self-centred and get ourselves into a course from which only God can redeem us. That is why we have the great act of incarnation: God's own redeeming presence in history through Jesus Christ. That is why God's presence goes on for ever in the hearts of his people through the Holy Spirit. This divine presence is available in a fuller form to everybody, everywhere, and in every age, through the Holy Spirit. Now, we know God as the

Father of our Lord Jesus Christ. Therefore we are free from any kind of fear. Love drives out fear. God is love.

Christianity and Diseases

It is generally believed that when a person becomes sick, God has chastised that person, because of a certain sin known or unknown. When a friend sees such a person, he will say, "We are only human beings, sinful as we are, and in many ways we make our heavenly Father angry, so that he whips us. May he, out of his own kindness and love, forgive you and may you be healed." So diseases are caused by God's anger against our sins. We know that an evil action may cause pain and even death. If you put honey in your eyes, you are bound to feel pain and not sweetness. Out of carelessness and a loose life many lives have been lost. He who does not care in driving a car, causes death to all the passengers. If you walk through a wild place by night, you may be bitten by a venomous snake and die. If you drive a car while drunk, you are bound to have an accident which will cause you pain and death. If you expose yourself to be bitten by mosquitoes, by ticks, rats, lice and fleas, you will be down with malaria, dengue, yellow fever, relapsing fever, typhus, filariasis etc. And if you do not care what you eat, what you wear, if you do not look after your house and your bed where you sleep, if your place is untidy and dirty, if you do not exercise your body, then you are bound to be ill and die before time. If you mean to say that God is angry because he gave you wisdom and knowledge to look after yourself, but you have not used these talents, one may understand why God's anger caused diseases. But usually, it seems as if we are responsible ourselves for some of the diseases when we become careless and lazy.

The usual rule is to take our friends or child, or wife or husband to the nearest hospital when he or she is ill. This is our duty as Christians; but there is a strong conception among the villagers that many more diseases are not for the hospital. The doctors do not know these diseases because:

45

a) they are caused by witchcraft and
b) because they are *Vimbuza*.[1] These are diseases which are to be healed by roots and drums.
c) and there are diseases which are healed by extracting blood out of the body.

There are diseases which can be healed by doctors in hospitals and there are diseases which can be healed only by soothsayers *(nchimi)*.

I do not accept the idea that there are Christian medicines and heathen medicines. I know of many so called African doctors (herbalists) who heal complicated and dangerous diseases. I know their names and their faces well. I feel that God gave these herbalists special gifts of healing. I do not accept the idea of European and African medicines at all. But I know that there are medicines to heal diseases. People die in the hospitals as well as in the hands of herbalists.

Because of some of the above ideas among the villagers the sick person is brought into hospital too late to be healed. This means that the patient was first brought to a *nchimi* and when the relatives saw that their patient was at the point of death, then they took her or him to the hospital. Most of our relatives die at the door of a hospital. Where is the certainty of our Christianity here? Are we doing our duty as Christians? Is God, the God of love and care, the Father of our Lord Jesus Christ in whom we trust and have our being? Is God our loving Father or our cruel judge? The problem of pain and suffering is as old as the continent of Africa. Our belief is that God who created humanity and all things governs all things in his perfect, holy love. He looks after every human life in his gracious keeping. The whole course of what happens here is under the hands of God.

In connection with pain and suffering our Christian stand is on the teaching of the Bible, that evil and suffering is real; but that it is within the providence of God and can be overcome. But to say that

---

[1]   *Vimbuza* is the dance which cures a form of spirit possession among the Ngoni and Tumbuka in northern Malawi.

God himself inflicts evil and suffering upon his own creatures is far from the thoughts of most of us who are simple minded people.

Diseases, then, are caused by living creatures through bites of mosquitoes, fleas, rats etc., and through our carelessness. I know that we are reluctant to accept this point for we are influenced by our own up-bringing to point our fingers away from ourselves and say "so and so has caused the death of our relative because...."

Poverty, distress and sickness will never cease so long as this world lasts (Mark 13:19). We are God's sons and daughters. If among us there are some people who are under the guidance of God, they are already in his hands though they are in this world which is alienated from God. Our Lord has all authority from heaven and he is *in* his Church, and *with* his Church. There is therefore nothing to separate us from him who loves us, not even death itself. We have a leader who has conquered pain and diseases before us. Can we fear? God himself will take us to where He is. Not disease, not nature, not death, but he who has kept us here and walked with us. We have to trust in the faithfulness of God and his love.

Let us try to examine our Christian background. What does it tell us in connection with diseases? We need to ask the New Testament about this. It seems that in the time of Jesus Christ, it was believed that all sickness and physical diseases and pain were penalties imposed on people as the result of sin. Demons were concerned with all human suffering. The demons, if offended, avenged themselves by sending different forms of diseases (John 9:2). Our Lord Jesus Christ gave no sanction to any such idea of disease. He took time to combat these ancient superstitions. High fever seems to have been attributed by implication to an agency, and Jesus is said to have rebuked the fever. This probably was a reflection of the current conceptions (Luke 4:38-39). Our Lord was a Jew, and as such, he took time to act against the common belief of the people in regard to disease. Such beliefs on the causes of disease have been common among ancient peoples. These ideas prevailed with considerable force in later Judaism. The New Testament reflects the ideas of a time when the older conceptions were breaking up, but had not yet disappeared.

Human beings are naturally conservative. We keep our old beliefs and fears which prevailed before Christianity. We are there to fill up the sufferings of our Lord. Let us be strong and patient under the strong hand of God.

Christianity and Customs

Our customs are far too many, bad and good ones. We should only thank God in Christ that Christianity's influence upon bad customs has achieved its best results so far. The historical Christian church has with all its faults and sins, been an aid to our happiness and living, to our learning and awakening of our conscience to what is good and true and beautiful, converted cruel customs and rules to suit us and our position as at our contemporary stage. Women would accept this without question, when they remember their own position in the then society and their separation from public affairs, their subordinate status and inferiority.

To mention a few of the bad customs, one would mention the burial of chiefs or heads of the clans. It was a custom to bury with them some of their servants and wives. These servants and wives were buried alive to serve the chiefs in the under-world and to maintain their dignity there.

In some tribes a daughter-in-law covers herself, hiding her face from her father-in-law. She could hide even from her father-in-law's grave or any possession her father-in-law handles, such as spear or axe or stick. She cannot utter a word to her father-in-law. Until now, in other villages daughters-in-law are supposed to hide themselves from their husbands' parents and this is regarded as honour and loyalty to them.

Children should not share food with older people. They, children, must eat what is left over. If the parents were good they gave food to their children by hands not on wooden plates at all.

Until now in other districts, when a child is born, the older woman must shave the little baby before men see it, and put powder of charcoal on the centre of the child's head. Men are not supposed to see the baby before ten days.

There was no freedom among the family. The father had all the power over his sons and daughters of every age. What the son earned was for the father. It was as good as paternal power over children in the Roman period. This included marriage for it was the father who chose a wife for his son. The son had to obey without question.

Only men were heirs to their parents' property after death. This custom has to do with the patrilineal system of marriage among the Tumbuka people, unlike the Achewa who were matrilineal. Of course, in Christianity, proper marriage is the builder of society. Our Lord attached the highest sanctity to marriage and taught the exceeding strictness of the tie. He allowed no cause but unfaithfulness, or equivalent moral evil, to be a cause of separation. Marriage is a mystical union of the most holy and ennobling character. The great Christian idea behind it is that the body is "the temple of the Holy Spirit", and marriage is like the union of Christ with the souls of his followers. Christ Himself evidently felt the bond as one which more than any other binds human society together.

Among the tribes in the north of Malawi and beyond, there is the custom of paying *lobola* which is a sign of gratification and thankfulness as well as honour to the parents of the girl. Originally nobody paid *lobola* when marrying a slave-girl or elephant tusks when marrying a common girl. I do not say that it is a good custom or a bad one; but that it is a custom in the patrilineal system of marriage and for years people have followed it.

The subordination of women, however, seems to me to remain in the blood veins of the society, though it is beginning now to change. One sign is the continuation of polygamy amongst us. How possible would it be for a man who is married to court a woman, able and educated; and how possible would it be for the woman to accept this man with full knowledge of the other wife before her? As we all know there has been conflict in such polygamous marriages because love (*philos*) cannot be divided into two or three. It is love to the woman who is united with you into one body, not two or three.

Now, let us turn to the other side of the coin, where we see the following benefits in the customs. There is courtesy of women towards men. You notice women bowing down to greet someone, speaking politely in their soft voices. You notice politeness and loyalty of children to their parents no matter what age they may be, from twenty to forty years. This is where Malawians gain a high reputation among visitors and it is a glorious gift from God himself. This gives honour to everyone, not only parents, or those in authority over us, but also everyone who is older and responsible. You will notice that young people do not talk when they share food with elders. Sometimes you wonder how a young man takes off his axe from his shoulder in respect to elders. Daughters who are fully grown will never enter into their parents bed-room. And above all, if the family is well brought up, silence will be observed at worship.

In the society, when one dies, parents or relatives who are left have to find food and meat to feed their dear friends and relatives from far, who have come to share sorrow with them. When these come to condole their relatives, they bring with them gifts of money, goats or even cattle and food to help those many people who have gathered there. The church in Karonga area has stopped this custom, because it was forcing the poor people to bring in cattle and it was also connected with ancestral spirits. But in most places the custom is maintained because it helps the bereaved to feed the guests. The Christians from Karonga who are strictly loyal to their decision, do not eat meat at funerals even if they are far away from Karonga.

Well, does Christianity fit into all these customs? No other nation can answer this question for us. One knows that many customs which were good, became Christianized among people in other nations, such as Christmas celebrations etc. So customs and cultures are the things which other nations cannot criticise without previous knowledge of the nation.

Care should be taken in these customs. Let us not be complacent and say that because these customs are from our ancestors, therefore they are all good and useful. Some of these customs are notoriously bad and do not fit into our developing world. Others are dangerous in regard to Christianity such as the birth of twins and some customs in connection with the birth of a child while the father is away![2] The burning and throwing away of the body of an aborted baby. All these are cruel customs. We cannot keep them simply because they were customs from our forefathers.

Christianity and Marriage

Here we are putting our hands upon one of the most important issues in the whole make-up of the nations in every land. Having served the Church for 38 years as a pastor, I have conducted around 900 weddings amongst different tribes in different parts of the Northern and Central Regions of Malawi but out of this number only a few marriages still stand. There was a young man and a young woman at Mlowe who married on Friday and on Friday the following week the marriage was dissolved. The kirk session of the church tried to reconcile these two, but in vain. No reason was given for it at all. There are some who live together as wife and husband in body, but they are already separated in their hearts. No one cares for the other and life is really miserable. Children grow up in such an environment. What a pity!

True marriage springs from love, but for the marriage to be stable and firm, it must be based upon fidelity. Fidelity guarantees the permanence of the marriage which is the mysterious relation between man and woman. "God created man in his own image, male and female created he them". So there is no question of a woman being inferior. Marriage is not just a natural phenomenon, but an act which is based upon the foundation of natural occurrence. It only exists where the divine order of marriage is recognised as binding in itself, and the two persons are aware of this bond. Marriage then is,

---

[2]   It was traditionally taboo to have twins since this was considered a bad omen. Therefore when twins were born they were both thrown into a river or deep pit (*mbuna*).

from the ethical point of view, an order and an institution, based upon the will of God. As husband and wife, with their different structure and their different functions, are one in the physical fact of sexual union, they are therefore one in all their life together. They are one in all they do and are, for one another. Time itself has witnessed to this when we see with our eyes man and woman doing exactly the same things. Both are becoming "like angels in heaven." They both go out to work for their living. For the temporal elements belong to this earth, and ultimate ones belong to eternity. It is therefore not only sex, but companionship.

When the idea of marriage is not understood, the standard of morality goes down, the nation become unstable and weak, unable to stand for the truth. We learn this from the emphasis our Lord laid on marriage bonds. He said, "For your hardness of heart Moses wrote you this commandment. But from the beginning of creation, 'God made them male and female'. For this reason a man shall leave his father and mother and be joined to his wife and the two shall become one. So they are no longer two but one. What therefore God has joined together, let not man put asunder." (Mark 10:5-9).

When the writer was doing some research in 1972-1974, he came across a certain Church Constitution which was very argumentative. This Constitution dealt with monogamous and polygamous marriages, and argued that people are not going to be saved because of one wife of more wives. One failed to see where such an argument would come from. No one, so far had ever connected marriage with salvation, whether because of one wife or many wives. A woman is a person like any other person and therefore cannot be doubled for serving one man. One finds it difficult to find scriptural warrant for contracting a second or third wife to one man in the church. We know that David and Solomon in the Old Testament had many wives. We also know that Abraham was not at peace with his first wife after the birth of Isaac, so much so that he was forced by the circumstances to send away both his second wife and her son. But over and above this, these Old Testament leaders were not Christians. If we are loyal and sincere to Christ and follow Him as our Lord and God we shall hold true responsibility to our husbands and wives as Christian society ought to be. We thank God who "so loved the world that he gave his only Son that whoever believed in him should not perish but have eternal life." (John 3:16)

In regard to children, it is true that children are the crown of marriage for sexual intercourse and procreation. We fulfil the work of God uniting in the order of creation. Though man is feeble and vague in many of his ways, yet God is still creating men and women through Him in completion of his work of creation. But it is not the only reason why people marry. We are not to go back into the brutal idea of regarding a woman as a "breeding machine". Sexual intercourse is also intended by the Creator as a means of expressing the love of married people for one another. Sterility is neither the cause for separation nor the disappointment of man and woman in their married life. It should not cause unhappiness in the bond of marriage at all, for children are the gifts of God in accordance with his will and wisdom.

It should also be taken into account that young men and women should think very seriously when they get married. They must be able to stand on their own feet economically and socially. They must plan about how to maintain their lives to keep themselves happy and strong without depending entirely on their parents or guardians. Of course, we have now come to a stage in this country where both wife and husband go out early in the morning to work and earn their living. This is an excellent idea; but it has to be founded upon fidelity as mentioned above. The two must trust each other and both must be trusted by our Lord Jesus Christ.

Let me mention one new problem here. I have had chances to travel in many countries both in Africa and Europe and have encountered what is known as "mixed marriage". Here I must confess that no solution has come to my mind yet. I know that the problems come from our differences not in colour, but in customs, culture and environment. I wish that people should feel free to marry, in a Christian way of course, anyone anywhere. But how can these practical problems be solved? I see that the two live peacefully and joyfully together, but when they join their relatives from both sides, one detects fear and dislike among the relatives. Language becomes a burden and little things like table manners, kinds of food, attitudes to people, condolence, approach to older people of both sides etc. How can these practical problems be solved? Perhaps we need more educated Africans, Europeans and Indians to help in this problem. Because as the world is gradually coming together such marriages are unavoidable.

Where is the place of Christianity in all this? Does Christianity fit into all this institution of marriage? I know that in the history of the Church the ascetics have influenced ideas of marriage. Now nobody can take away some of these ideas, they have become part and parcel of Christian marriage, e.g. asceticism within the marriage bond. But let us hope to grow and be guided by the Holy Spirit through the Word of God.

In marriage the choice must be taken both by the man and by the woman. The two persons must choose each other to live together for life, forsaking all others. If this is done, we know that it is God himself who has directed both of them to join in marriage. In such marriages the name of God is glorified by the character, stability and joy of the couple. The love of God will be expressed in patience and kindness and will endure all things. The husband will defend his wife and the wife will support and comfort her husband. Both of them will aim at the happiness of each other, and their family.

Christianity and Death

Death to us is *destruction* and not only the end of the life of the one who is dead, but also confusion of the whole of the clan or family. It cuts so deep into the soul that one cannot forget the shock it marks on the life of those who are left. It is the end of everything in that person departed. It is the disappearance of his or her face, voice, action. Death is cruel and tyrannical. Death is ruthless for it can take away the only son or daughter. Death is the last enemy which we fear most. Death retards the progress and development of a family, a clan, a tribe and indeed even a nation. A person dies and leaves children behind him, he does not help them or write to them.

54

According to the ancestors' faith, death is *not* the end of this life. But people who have gone in that other world, speak different languages and eat different foods. Though they are always near, yet they cannot be seen or touched. Though they need exactly the food and clothes which we eat and wear, yet all these are transformed into different food and clothes to suit their places where they live now. If they appear to eat our food, they must be seen in the form of snakes, or animals or birds. However, there are times when the departed can be seen in their proper forms in dreams. They have different names. They are known as *Vibanda*, *Mizguka*, *Sifukupuku*, etc. There are stories from the mines of South Africa where we hear that they may appear to relatives who are working in these mines and give them money or gold. Those who are given the wealth, are told to leave work and go home, but keeping everything secretly. All those who leave this world and go into the other world are transformed: the babies become young men and women, and the old become young. Life is more enjoyable there than in this present world of ours. Yet they are lost from this world. Death is the end.

But in Christianity, faith in Christ is faith in his resurrection. (Resurrection is different from survival which is a conception common to nearly all people.) As God raised his Son from the grave and the grave was left empty, therefore all who love and follow Jesus Christ, the Son of God, in spirit and in truth, will also be raised to eternal life. The dead really die. There is no question about it. We are part of nature. We must die. But because we transcend nature we actually fear death. We are the only creatures who know that one day we are to leave this world and enter the unknown. The Bible teaches us that humanity was made in the image of God and was put into permanent union with the Creator. But human beings wanted to be like their Creator. They failed to live independently and therefore they die because they have the same limitations of biological existence as any other part of the natural order. "The sting of death is sin" (1 Corinthians 15:56), and sin is to rebel against God. Death is a break with the past and a bridge to the future. It is final and life is short here on earth.

The dead really die. What Christianity teaches is to separate biological death from the death of the "I", the "me", the *ego* which does not die as long as a person is in Christ. "As in Adam all die, so in Christ shall all be made alive" (1 Corinthians 15:22). What has actually happened among all people on earth is this: the giant who terrified all races on earth has been completely conquered by the most powerful giant. The giant who was called Mr Death has been killed by this most powerful giant whose name is Christ.

This is to be compared with a dangerous lion which killed many people in olden days. One brave and strong man killed it. People were still fearing the animal, the story of the animal's death was believed by a few people who were saved from the terror of the lion and lived at peace. But the majority of people who did not believe in the story of the conquest of this old lion were still living under the shadow of fear. They feared the lion which was already dead and rotten. So, this is like men and women today who do not believe in Jesus Christ. To them death is before them and very near. The fear of this death causes terrible blindness and ignorance. They wander about in search of anyone or anything that would save them from death which is both to kill the body as well as the spirit or the ego. The fear of this old dead lion has caused manifold fears. They fear their fellow man and they fear truth itself. All this is deep down in their conscience. But to those who believe in Christ and his resurrection, death is dead and left behind. They are at peace and enjoy this present life with Him who conquered death. For a person who is constantly in God's presence, who is conscious that God has held his hand all his life, and who is sure that He will guide him to the end, cannot believe that death is the end. "Thou dost guide me with thy counsel, and afterward thou will receive me to glory." (Psalm 73:24) When we listen to Jesus' argument to the Sadducees, he said, "You do not know the power of God" (Mark 12:24). The future is bright only when the reality of communion with the living God is assured. In him it is life which has the last word, not death. God, the Father of our Lord Jesus Christ, will not allow the communion which began on earth to be ended by death. He means his children to enjoy the life of the kingdom now. The future is in his hands. His grace and power are known here. God *is*. He does not say that he *was* Abraham's God. No. God *is*. In Jesus Christ God acted with power to bring life and immortality to light. So a Christian may get into trouble, pain and death, but life of high quality which cannot be destroyed has begun, here and now, for all who will receive it as an important gift from him who entered humanity in the fullness of the time. So that whether we live or die, we are the Lord's. To the Christian, death is left behind! The Christian faith has a God who knew his way out of the grave.

Our Lord said, "He that believes in me, *has* eternal life. So believing in Christ is life itself, eternal life. Eternal life begins where fellowship with Christ begins. When Christ comes into a person's life, doubt must disappear. Christ and doubt cannot exist together Christ alone can overcome our doubt. Christ alone can really free us from the fear of death. In doing that Christ makes us joyful people. "In the world you shall have tribulation, but be of good cheer, for I have overcome the world" (John 16:33). Jesus Christ said that he has overcome our fear by standing beside us. Here is the gift of salvation in Jesus Christ - from doubt, from tribulation and from death itself.

Jesus says very little on the subject of physical death. You can detect something from when he said, "She is not dead but sleeping" (Matthew 9:24; Mark 5:39; Luke 8:52). He knew that our true being is something apart from mere bodily existence. Death thus took its course as a natural incident, analogous to sleep, which broke the continuity of life only in appearance. Listen to what our Lord said to his disciples: "Fear not them that kill the body, and after that have no more that they can do..." (Luke 12:4; Matthew 10:28). Life resides in the soul, over which God alone has power. The accident of death, of the separation of the soul from its material body, can make little difference to the essential human being.

So why go to Simon Magus? Please go to Jesus Christ! He will make you rest and live for ever in the spiritual body.

Christianity and the Churches

A few fisher-men, simple people, having followed our Lord Jesus Christ, and seen with their own eyes the mighty work done by Jesus, formed an organisation whose members were nicknamed "Christians" at Antioch. Having received the promised divine power in the name of the Holy Spirit, they founded Christianity. This was the beginning of the Catholic Church of Christ, which later was divided into the Eastern Orthodox Communion and the Roman Church. Then there appeared churches of the East, Copts and Armenians, Jacobites and Assyrians. Then followed another division in northern and western Europe between the churches of the Reformation and the Roman Catholic Church. The Protestant churches further divided into two types - Lutheran and Reformed or Calvinist. In England there came division between the Anglican Communion and the various Free Churches. These dispersed into North America and elsewhere throughout the English speaking world. We have also further denominations such as Quakers, Salvationists, Seventh-Day Adventists, Latter-Day Saints and many more. These churches have a variety of confessions, creeds and doctrines.

Thank God that Christianity does not consist merely of a set of convictions regarding abstract truth. It is, by the common confession of all its adherents, first and foremost a way of life, lived in union with and allegiance to a Person - Jesus Christ. There is, as Christ has revealed to us, one God, infinitely wise, powerful, merciful, loving and holy. There is no other God but he in whom is found righteousness, loving-kindness, transcendence, and majestic uniqueness, as taught in the Bible.

There is diversity of belief among Christians, but the things to which all agree are many more than those about which they differ. In common they have the Bible through which God has revealed himself to us, the knowledge of God as our Father only in Christ through the Holy Spirit, and confidence in God's purpose of redemption through the life and death of Jesus Christ.

One is not capable of continuing with this common church history which has been handed over to us by learned people of old. But let us turn our attention to the attitude of present village society to other churches, which did not start long ago. One would not mention the names of the churches in question, but suffice to say that the first thing you notice in the village is the enmity between these little groups of so-called churches and the historical churches. Of course, there was a time in which, even these historical churches were rivals and contradicted to each offer. But now with the help of the Spirit of Jesus Christ there has arisen the Ecumenical Movement (*oikoumene*) which is drawing all the churches together. I am not imagining or thinking of the false utopian idea of one world-wide church of Christ. No, I am thinking of the fellowship which enables each member Church to speak and act freely as partakers together with Christ. Here we speak the truth of one faith, which points to one way to the heavenly Father, namely Jesus Christ his only Son. In this we are to meet our brother and our sister - both as a Christian and as a human being. We know that Christ himself goes before us.

Let me come back to the point I made of hatred and tensions between the historical churches and the new churches. In my own experience I have more than once come across a group of people quarrelling and exchanging insults: "You are a Satanic church, and we are the Christian church etc." If it is at a burial place and the dead man or woman belongs to CCAP, no one from another group will even shut his eyes or say "Amen" to prayers or even come near the graveyard. If it is the other group's death the whole preaching will be directed against CCAP or Roman Catholic Church or any other historical church if they happen to be present.

In the villages people do not really understand the importance of unity and especially unity in Christ. The church of Christ is one and, like a house, it has many rooms, some big and others small. The owner knows these rooms and cares for them. "Let them grow together," said our Lord (Matthew 13:30).

I know that in many parts of the world we Christians must be careful lest we entangle ourselves in what is called "syncretism". This we do fear, but fear should not lead us into hatred and quarrelling. If we do this, how can we carry out our commission as Christians to convert those who are outside Christ's control? For the name of church is not going to save anyone! Christ saves! We are not the judges to judge our fellow human beings. Christ is the sole judge of our lives. Christianity is love of Christ to all men and women. If we as Christians hate others because they belong to other churches from ours, or because they are outside the church, we surely do not represent the spirit of our Lord at all. If we love them as fellow human beings, we may open their eyes to learn and see the love of Christ for themselves and so enable them to come to Christ and his salvation. Remember that, by the standard of the moral life of Christ, we are all sinners; but let us as sinners humbly offer ourselves sincerely to be cleansed in which process our fellow human beings will follow our example.

Division in the churches need not hinder us from serving our fellow human beings. Should the structure of a church move to people, or should people move to the structure? In olden days people used to walk long distances to go to where churches were. Maybe the time has now come that the churches walk to the people on Sundays! For Sunday is a day of joy and freedom and the gospel is to serve the people. Our Lord was always and is always with his people where they are, to draw them to himself for he came "to seek and to save that which was lost" (Luke 19:10).

Why is it that there are tensions and squabbles between churches in Christianity? Let us examine ourselves. Within our own denominations we have not safeguarded our own personal moral standard as being examples of Christ's disciples. Forgive me for saying that our moral standard as Christian ministers, elders, deacons and Christians in general in the Church of Central Africa Presbyterian, has actually gone *down* very badly indeed. Well, how can we point with our finger at someone who is superstitious, if we too fear the unknown? How can we encourage our friend to take his child to the hospital, if we ourselves have no belief in the doctors and instead our eyes are fixed on a witchdoctor? How can we criticise bad customs, if we go in rags after the birth of our own twins, and smear black clay on top of the grave of our own dear ones to chase away witches? How can we comfort the bereaved, if we ourselves add to their sorrow by telling them untruthfully that somebody came by night and took away the dead body for meat? We very often encourage the bereaved to go and see Simbazako[3] or a witchfinder. How can we help our people in their attitude to other denominations if we are always in our speech and life looking down on other churches as Satanic!

If we were being sincere to our Lord, we would be accused of being revolutionary and turning this world up-side-down (Acts 17:6). We belong to Christ. Let us be honest and ask ourselves whether we first love God and truly serve Christ who has called us out of darkness into his wonderful light. Let us help our fellow human beings if we ourselves have been helped by our Lord Jesus Christ. Let us be open to everybody so that we can learn the truth of our Lord. We know that we will be accused of pride and even be hated by our own relatives. But, at the end, Christ will take us to his side. Can other persons see the presence of Christ in us? Let us be true and honest to God, to others and to ourselves in all that we are. Let us try to find out the good side of others and help them to grow speaking the truth in love.

Christianity and the churches are two different things. We can have the church which we have organised and put a label of the name of "Christ" on it. It can live for sometime, but not for ever. Christianity was founded by Christ himself and as such it must follow Christ and live according to his will. His will is the salvation of all people here on earth. Christianity banishes all pride and cunning, all selfishness and worldly wisdom for it belongs to Christ himself whose cross was a stumbling block to the Jews and foolishness to the Greeks. We are only his servants in all what we do in his Christian church. The weakness which was seen at Christ's cross is the power and wisdom of God for our salvation.

Christianity and the World

Christianity is here in this beautiful and wonderful world of ours which God created for us men and women to live in and develop. The

---

3   A well-known healer and witchfinder.

world in which we must live and learn to be the children of God. If we really obey the Creator and act in accordance with his will, then we may enjoy the real and greatest freedom and happiness, in which pain, sorrow and sufferings are shared with his Son Jesus Christ who has conquered them all.

God loves this world. This is shown in many passages of the Scripture. This is why he gave his only begotten Son to redeem it from the slavery of sin. The kingdom of God is here and now. It is growing secretly until God shall reign for ever and ever. According to Jesus Christ's priestly prayer, we are here in this world, but we are not *of* this world (John 17:14). Paul says, "But our citizenship is in heaven" (Philippians 3:20). So this beautiful world of ours is our training ground for each one of us to enjoy God's freedom through different channels. This freedom means that we, as God's creatures, insist on being human as God meant us to be - to realise and express our own human nature and to achieve, under God's own guidance and care, the fulfilment of our own unique personal destiny. Failing this, we lose our humanity.

The kingdom of God which is the rule of God in the hearts of men and women is a relation between God as King and us as his subjects. The relation is maintained by what God does to us and what we do to God. In other words, it consists of the contributions of both God and ourselves. As King, God offers protection, guidance and a way of life. God is King in an absolute sense for he does all these things without change. God is not capricious. On our side, the contribution is what God requires from us: loyalty, trust and obedience. God alone as King is our protector, guide and legislator, whose rule of life is summed up in complete loyalty, trust and obedience towards the King.

Loyalty to God, if it is to be true and sincere, must mean here the loss of friends, relatives, personal liberty, property and even life itself. For to share the glory of the King in future, we must begin now when we can share the present Christ's humiliations and sufferings, bringing people to his kingdom.

Our Lord Jesus Christ represents the kingdom of his Father here on earth. He is here to persuade men and women to come into a banquet which his Father has prepared for them. Our Lord complained that while the kingdom is already here, men and women do not obey the call to enter into it. Jesus being the servant of all is the chief. He is the leader fighting alone against the whole kingdom of evil. He is there to offer complete obedience to his Father who makes him King of Kings, and Lord of Lords. The cross where Jesus suffered, opens the kingdom of God to men and women. His death has accomplished what Jesus really wanted God's world to be. The battle has been fought and won at the cross. Christ shall subdue all enemies of his heavenly kingdom and hand over the kingdom of his Father.

Therefore the kingdom of God here in this world of ours means that people are wholly devoted to God as their King and serve God in spreading his kingdom all over the world, not by force of arms, but by his spiritual power. This kingdom, according to the Servant Songs, is not to be an earthly empire. No, it is to bring men and women under God's rule in their hearts, not by forcing them to accept it, but by persuading them to accept God as their sole King.

What does village society think of this world? Probably they think of it as a place where we all suffer pain and tribulation. A ruthless place full of hardship. A place where there is no rest and no real peace. It is an egg where we live closed inside, and when we die, we climb on a long ladder to join our relatives who are up there in the skies. This idea is a new one, introduced after the coming of Christianity. Up there, it is believed, there is no hoeing or cutting trees or building houses. When we reach there, we shall rest by sitting on comfortable places. There is no poverty, or diseases, or pain and suffering, or war, or ignorance, or under age or over age. It is a place where everybody else who enters it is clean and smart, wearing white robes and always happy and gay. This world is cursed by the Creator because the chameleon was too slow to report to the Creator and so death came in. This world is a place where only rich people and mighty people live comfortably and at peace such as *Bazungu* (Europeans). The noun seems to come from *kuzungula*, meaning "to loosen". The *Bazungu* are loosened from all hardship and difficulties. Therefore in this world one has to be clever enough and careful when he tames cattle or goats etc. He must put in certain medicine to protect them from witches, lions and hyenas. He must also do the same to safeguard his house and his family. In connection with this belief, when someone's boy or girl fails to pass his or her examinations, some parents have even gone to a witchdoctor to look for medicine to enable the boy or the girl to pass his or her examinations. There is always a cause for anything that happens in this world. One man had his house built and covered with corrugated iron sheets near my house. One day in 1979 a strong wind blew off the iron sheets from the house. He accused his relatives of having done this! He has now moved away from that village. But his house was built of unburned bricks.

What a world is this that allows bad people to do damage to their neighbours. These bad people are thought to have power to tame lions and hyenas in order to destroy someone's cattle and goats. But these bad men are not supposed to tame cattle and goats by the same power! This world is full of evil men. Is this God's world? Is this the world under the control of God as the only King, if everybody else can divert the wind and the lion and the snake to kill his neighbour. How can Christianity, which is Christ, make us free? What freedom is this if we are surrounded by all sorts of powers over us? Is there any truth in all these terrible and dreadful stories? If we from our youth believe that there is some truth in these, how can such truth make us free in this beautiful world which is our training ground? "If you continue in my word, you are truly my disciples," said Jesus, "and you will know the truth, and the truth will make you free" (John 8:31-32). God has an absolute claim over us, and over this world he created, and there is no other power over God's creation. One does not know and claim to know all the causes of calamities that happen here in this world. But God knows.

Our ancestors used to say that the world means men and women. The trouble is that we cannot allow ourselves to understand others in this world. To understand, to me, means to accept one's attitude as it stands without judging it first. We seem to be afraid and try to defend ourselves. When we are defensive, fear begins to come out of nothing whatsoever. Friends become enemies and good people become bad. We know that we are not ants which are all the same.

64

We must differ. There are times when we must agree to differ. But to differ from a friend is not to make enmity between the two. Let us also avoid being taken up by empty praises of others. Be yourself in Christ, and seek to be honest, thorough, open and sound. We human beings are the same in our deep feelings, and remember that no-one is wholly bad or wholly good. Therefore honesty with ourselves and with others is most rewarding, both here and here-after. The motto is: say what you mean and mean what you say. Be what you are. Then this world of ours would be what Christ meant it to be.

The peace of Jesus Christ be with us all, and let us, in our hearts, allow Christ to teach us and judge us, so that this beautiful world of ours should be a home where we live happily as Christians in Christianity.

Christianity and the Future

Theologians have already helped us to know something about the future. So I am not attempting to write on eschatology, or final judgement, or the Christian hope at all. What I intend to write here is the future of Christianity as far as village society is concerned. What is the future of Christianity in this country? The question is difficult, but it can be answered from both the past and the present way of life of Christians.

Let us take Jesus Christ from whom we have Christianity. He was not one of the Pharisees nor a Rabbi. He was a child of the people. He stood upon the side of the the vast toiling classes. His power over the multitude was due in part to the fact that he stood in support of the common people and helped them to receive the kingdom of his Father. He was the true friend of tax-collectors and sinners; and the result of his teaching was their social emancipation. He redeemed labour in his own person. He made the worker of whatever grade the true aristocrat. Idleness and selfishness were sins against society. Jesus discarded the mischievous delusion that the highest state of humanity is to sit with folded hands on a splendid sofa. He asserted that the life that is not helpful is hateful. He asserted the moral might of meekness and the true glory of humility. If you help your neighbour heartily, you really love God. Christ taught and gave example of sacrifice. He taught that the highest glory of humanity is the power of sacrificing oneself for another. There is no real nobility, but at the price of sacrifice. Love is sacrifice, patriotism is sacrifice, holiness is sacrifice. "Go and sell all your possessions and give them to the poor" (Matthew 19:21). The Lord's own example is his own cross upon which our salvation depends. Sacrifice is not a bitter necessity of life, but a splendid right and privilege. For only a human being could conceive the thought of dying for his fellows.

But looking at what the Christian church is and does in the villages, the future is dark. The moral standard is low. The truth itself is feared. To trust in the Lord is probably to shout his name in the pulpit through the mouth while the heart is far away from him who called us. We shall do little to elevate people if our words are mocked by the meanness of our lives. The world is refusing, and rightly so, to be stirred by the counsels of those who preach nobility but neglect to practise it; who declare the glory of unselfishness while their own lives are tainted by self seeking; and who preach the nobility of self-denial, while their own hearts are the altars of Mammon. Preaching against adultery in order to have all women to themselves!

Christianity here is like an old car with rotten brakes, and the car is going down the hill to cross a rotten bridge. Someone asks, "What is the future of Christianity in the villages?" If Christianity in this is compared with the old car and the old bridge - the answer to the question is obvious! Indeed, to expect perfection in others is absurd, when we are so deeply conscious of imperfection in ourselves.

From faith in Christ, Christianity will never end. Christ himself said, "I tell you, if these were silent, the very stones would cry out" (Luke 19:40). Christianity is to stay, but you and me are to be lost in the wilderness of despair and sorrow. Eternal life is here and now in Jesus Christ and him alone. Christ was raised from the dead and he is alive in and with his church. If we are to think of our future, the world is the battle-ground of good and evil and the training place of the children of God. It awaits the day when all wrong will be put right and truth will prevail.

Christianity means a great deal to us all. It means that we become examples of good citizenship in our country. It means honesty and truthfulness in all our dealings with others. It means serving God in serving our neighbour. It means our right-relation with God and therefore with our neighbour which means righteousness. It means justice and sincerity throughout our lives in all our actions, words and thoughts. It means love (*agape*) to all people. It means kindness and generosity. It means faithfulness. It means happiness and courage. It means openness and frankness. It means reasonableness and orthodoxy. Christianity means trust in our heavenly Father, the Father of our Lord Jesus Christ. It means living the life of Christ. Christianity is Christ.

67